1935 if you wanted to
read a good book, you needed
either a lot of money or a library card.
Cheap paperbacks were available, but their
poor production generally mirrored the quality
between the covers. One weekend that year,
Allen Lane, Managing Director of The Bodley Head,
having spent the weekend visiting Agatha Christie,
found himself on a platform at Exeter station trying to
find something to read for his journey back to London.
He was appalled by the quality of the material he had to
choose from. Everything that Allen Lane achieved from that
day until his death in 1970 was based on a passionate belief
in the existence of 'a vast reading public for *intelligent*
books at a low price'. The result of his momentous vision
was the birth not only of Penguin, but of the 'paperback
revolution'. Quality writing became available for the price of
a packet of cigarettes, literature became a mass medium
for the first time, a nation of book-borrowers became a
nation of book-buyers – and the very concept of book
publishing was changed for ever. Those founding
principles – of quality and value, with an overarching
belief in the fundamental importance of reading –
have guided everything the company has
done since 1935. Sir Allen Lane's
pioneering spirit is still very much alive
at Penguin in 2005. Here's to
the next 70 years!

MORE THAN A BUSINESS

'We decided it was time to end the almost customary half-hearted manner in which cheap editions were produced – as though the only people who could possibly want cheap editions must belong to a lower order of intelligence. We, however, believed in the existence in this country of a vast reading public for intelligent books at a low price, and staked everything on it'
Sir Allen Lane, 1902–1970

'The Penguin Books are splendid value for sixpence, so splendid that if other publishers had any sense they would combine against them and suppress them'
George Orwell

'More than a business … a national cultural asset'
Guardian

'When you look at the whole Penguin achievement you know that it constitutes, in action, one of the more democratic successes of our recent social history'
Richard Hoggart

The Coronation of Haile Selassie

EVELYN WAUGH

PENGUIN BOOKS

PENGUIN BOOKS

Published by the Penguin Group
Penguin Books Ltd, 80 Strand, London WC2R ORL, England
Penguin Group (USA) Inc., 375 Hudson Street, New York, New York 10014, USA
Penguin Group (Canada), 10 Alcorn Avenue, Toronto, Ontario, Canada M4V 3B2
(a division of Pearson Penguin Canada Inc.)
Penguin Ireland, 25 St Stephen's Green, Dublin 2, Ireland
(a division of Penguin Books Ltd)
Penguin Group (Australia), 250 Camberwell Road, Camberwell, Victoria 3124,
Australia (a division of Pearson Australia Group Pty Ltd)
Penguin Books India Pvt Ltd, 11 Community Centre,
Panchsheel Park, New Delhi – 110 017, India
Penguin Group (NZ), cnr Airborne and Rosedale Roads, Albany,
Auckland 1310, New Zealand (a division of Pearson New Zealand Ltd)
Penguin Books (South Africa) (Pty) Ltd, 24 Sturdee Avenue,
Rosebank 2196, South Africa

Penguin Books Ltd, Registered Offices: 80 Strand, London WC2R ORL, England

www.penguin.com

Remote People first published by Gerald Duckworth and Company Ltd 1931
Published in Penguin Books 1985
This extract published as a Pocket Penguin 2005

1

Set in 11/13pt Monotype Dante
Typeset by Palimpsest Book Production Limited
Polmont, Stirlingshire
Printed in England by Clays Ltd, St Ives plc

Contents

The Coronation of Haile Selassie

It is to *Alice in Wonderland* that my thoughts recur in seeking some historical parallel for life in Addis Ababa. There are others: Israel in the time of Saul, the Scotland of Shakespeare's *Macbeth*, the Sublime Porte as one sees it revealed in the dispatches of the late eighteenth century, but it is in *Alice* only that one finds the peculiar flavour of galvanized and translated reality, where animals carry watches in their waistcoat pockets, royalty paces the croquet lawn beside the chief executioner, and litigation ends in a flutter of playing-cards. How to recapture, how retail, the crazy enchantment of these Ethiopian days?

First let me attempt to convey some idea of the setting. Addis Ababa is a new town; so new, indeed, that not a single piece of it appears to be really finished. Menelik the Great chose the site forty years ago and named it, when it was still a hillside encampment, 'The New Flower'. Till then the Government had shifted between the ancient, priest-ridden cities of the north, mobile according to the exigencies of fuel, but morally centred on Axum, the ecclesiastical capital, as the French monarchy centred on Rheims. Menelik was the first king to break the tradition of coronation at Axum, and at the time even his vast military prestige suffered from the breach. It is mentioned by contemporary writers as a source of weakness; actually it was a necessary part of his policy. He was no longer merely king of the Christian, Amharic highlanders, he was emperor of a great territory embracing in the west the black pagan Shankallas, in the east the nomad anthropophagous Danakils, in the south-east the Ogaden desert inhabited by Somalis, and in the south the great belt of cultivable land held by the Mohammedan Gallas. At Addis Ababa he found the new centre for his possessions, still in the highlands among his own people, but on their extreme edge; immediately at its foot lies the territory of the wretched Guratchi, the despised, ill-conditioned people who provide the labour for building and sweeping; Hawash is the land of the Gallas. Addis Ababa is the strategic point for the control of these discordant dominions. Lej Yasu contemplated a further, more radical change. It appears to have been his purpose, or the purpose of his counsellors, to reorientate the empire from Harar and build up a great Mohammedan Power which should in the event of the victory of the Central Powers in Europe, enclose the whole Somali coastline. It was an intemperate ambition which needed no European intervention to encompass its downfall. The exact circumstances of his failure may, perhaps, never be known, nor the extent to which these plans were even clearly formulated. It is certain that he was in correspondence with the Mad Mullah in British Somaliland. It is widely believed that he had in his last years frankly apostatized from the Church; his father's Mohammedan origin added colour to this report, and proof was supplied in the form of his portrait wearing a turban which purported to have been taken at Harar.

Many, however, declare that this conclusive piece of evidence was fabricated in Addis Ababa by an Armenian photographer. Whatever the truth of these details, the fact is clear that the unfortunate young man fell, not, as is usually said, through his grosser habits of life, which, indeed, tended rather to endear him to his humbler subjects, but through his neglect of what must remain for many years to come the strength of the Ethiopian Empire – its faith and the warlike qualities of the Amharic hillsmen. Lej Yasu has not been seen since 1916. He is said to be living, listless and morbidly obese, under Ras Kassa's guardianship at Fiche, but a traveller who lately passed the reputed house of his captivity remarked that the roof was out of repair and the entrance overgrown with weeds. People do not readily speak of him, for the whole country is policed with spies, but more than one European who enjoyed the confidence of his servants told me that the name is still greatly respected among the lower orders. He has, through his mother, the true blood of Menelik. They describe him as a burly young man with compelling eyes, recklessly generous and superbly dissipated. Tafari's astute diplomacy strikes some of them as far less kingly.

There was no constitution in Ethiopia. The succession was determined in theory by royal proclamation, in practice by bloodshed. Menelik had left no male and no legitimate children. Lej Yasu's mother was his daughter and he had nominated Lej Yasu. In the circumstances, Lej Yasu had named no successor and there was thus no indisputable heir. By right of Menelik's blood, his second daughter reigned as the Empress Zauditu, but her religious duties occupied more of her attention than the routine of government. A regent was necessary; three or four noblemen had, by descent, equal claims to the office. The most important of these was Ras Kassa, but deeply concerned with religion and the management of his estates, he was unambitious of wider obligations. The danger which confronted the country was that Menelik's conquests would again disintegrate into a handful of small kingdoms, and that the imperial throne would become a vague overlordship. In such a condition, Abyssinian independence could scarcely hope to survive the penetration of European commercial interests. The rases appreciated the position and realized that there was only one man whose rank, education, intellect, and ambition qualified him for the throne. This was Ras Tafari. Accordingly, by their consent and choice, he became Negus. With the general public, outside his own provinces, his prestige was slight; he was distinguished neither by the blood of Menelik nor any ostentatious feat of arms. Among the rases he was *primus inter pares*; one of themselves chosen to do a job, and answerable to them for its satisfactory execution. From this precarious position in the years that followed, Tafari gradually built up and consolidated his supremacy. He travelled in Europe; he was at pains to impress visiting Europeans with his enlightenment. He played on the rivalries of the French and Italian representatives, and secured his own position at home by advancing his country's position in the world. He obtained admission to the League of Nations; everywhere he identified himself with his country, until Europe came to look to him as its natural ruler.

Even so, he had to fight for his throne. In the spring of 1930 a powerful noble named Ras Gougsa* rebelled. He was the husband of the empress; they had been divorced, but maintained cordial and intimate relations. Tafari's army was victorious, and, in the bloodthirsty rout, Gougsa was himself slain. The empress died suddenly next day, and Tafari, with the assent of the rases, proclaimed himself emperor, fixing for his coronation the earliest date by which preparations could adequately be made. The coronation festivities were thus the final move in a long and well-planned strategy. Still maintaining his double ruff of trumping at home with prestige abroad, abroad with his prestige at home, Tafari had two main motives behind the display. He wished to impress on his European visitors that Ethiopia was no mere agglomeration of barbarous tribes open to foreign exploitation, but a powerful, organized, modern State. He wanted to impress on his own countrymen that he was no paramount chiet of a dozen independent communities, but an absolute monarch recognized on equal terms by the monarchies and governments of the great world. And if, in the minds of any of his simpler subjects, courtesy and homage became at all confused, if the impression given was that these braided delegates (out for a holiday from their serious duties, an unusual pageant, and perhaps a few days' shooting) had come in their ruler's name to pay

* There is a Ras Gougsa, quite unconnected with the rebel, who is still living. He acted as host to the American delegation during the coronation.

tribute to Ethiopian supremacy – so much the better. The dismembered prisoners of Adowa were still unavenged. The disconcertingly eager response of the civilized Powers gave good colour to this pretension. 'We did not think so much of Tafari,' remarked the servant of one Englishman, 'until we learned that your king was sending his own son to the coronation'; and there can be no doubt that the other rases, confronted at close quarters with the full flood of European diplomacy, realized more clearly that other qualities were needed for the government of a modern State than large personal property and descent from Solomon. This very exuberance, however, of European interest tended to hinder the accomplishment of the emperor's first ambition. The gun-cases were his undoing, for in the days that followed the celebrations, when the delegations were scattered on safari about the interior of the country, they had the opportunity of observing more than had been officially prepared for them. They saw just how far the emperor's word ran in the more distant parts of his dominions; they saw the frail lines of communication which bound the Government to its outposts; they saw something of the real character of the people, and realized how inadequate an introduction to the national life were the caviare and sweet champagne of Addis Ababa.

I have said above that the coronation was fixed for the earliest date by which preparations could be made. This statement needs some qualification and brings me back from this political digression to the description of Addis

Ababa with which I began the chapter, for the first, obvious, inescapable impression was that nothing was ready or could possibly be made ready in time for the official opening of the celebrations six days hence. It was not that one here and there observed traces of imperfect completion, occasional scaffolding or patches of unset concrete; the whole town seemed still in a rudimentary stage of construction. At every corner were half-finished buildings; some had been already abandoned; on others, gangs of ragged Guraghi were at work. It is difficult to convey in words any real idea of the inefficiency to which low diet and ill-will had reduced these labourers. One afternoon I watched a number of them, twenty or thirty in all, under the surveillance of an Armenian contractor, at work clearing away the heaps of rubble and stone which encumbered the courtyard before the main door of the palace. The stuff had to be packed into wooden boxes swung between two poles, and emptied on a pile fifty yards away. Two men carried each load, which must have weighed very little more than an ordinary hod of bricks. A foreman circulated among them, carrying a long cane. When he was engaged elsewhere the work stopped altogether. The men did not sit down; chat, or relax in any way; they simply stood stock-still where they were, motionless as cows in a field, sometimes arrested with one small stone in their hands. When the foreman turned his attention towards them they began to move again, very deliberately, like figures in a slow-motion film; when he beat them they did not look round or remonstrate, but quickened their movements just perceptibly; when the blows

7

ceased they lapsed into their original pace until the foreman's back being turned, they again stopped completely. (I wondered whether the Pyramids were built in this way.) Work of this nature was in progress in every street and square of the town.

Addis Ababa extends five or six miles in diameter. It lies at a height of eight thousand feet, with a circle of larger hills to the north of it, culminating at Entoto in a mountain of about ten thousand. The station is at the southern extremity of the town, and from it a broad road leads up to the post office and principal commercial buildings. Two deep watercourses traverse the town, and round their slopes, and in small groves of eucalyptus scattered between the more permanent buildings, lie little clusters of *tukals*, round native huts, thatched and windowless. Down the centre of the main thoroughfares run metalled tracks for motor-traffic, bordered on either side by dust and loose stones for mules and pedestrians; at frequent intervals are sentry-boxes of corrugated iron, inhabited by drowsy, armed policemen; there are also police at point duty, better trained than most of the motor-drivers in European signals of control. Attempts are even made, with canes and vigorous exchanges of abuse, to regulate the foot-traffic, a fad which proves wholly unintelligible to the inhabitants. The usual way for an Abyssinian gentleman to travel is straight down the middle of the road on mule-back with ten or twenty armed retainers trotting all round him; there are continual conflicts between the town police and the followers of the country gentleman, from which the police often come out the worse.

Every man in Abyssinia carries arms; that is to say, he wears a dagger and bandoleer of cartridges round his waist and has a slave-boy walking behind with a rifle. There is some question about the efficacy of these weapons, which are mostly of some antiquity. Some are of the Martini type, probably salvaged from the field of Adowa, others are comparatively modern, bolt-action weapons and old, English service-rifles. They have percolated through singly from Somaliland and been brought in, disguised as other merchandise, by such romantic gun-runners as Arthur Rimbaud and M. de Montfried. Cartridges are a symbol of wealth and, in the interior, a recognized medium of exchange; their propriety for any particular brand of firearm is a matter of secondary importance; often the brass ammunition displayed in the bandoleers will not fit the rifle carried behind, and there is usually a large percentage of expended cartridges among it.

The streets are always a lively scene; the universal white costume being here and there relieved by the brilliant blues and violets of mourning or the cloaks of the upper classes. The men walk about hand in hand in pairs and little groups; quite often they are supporting some insensible drunkard. Women appear in the markets, but take no part in the general street-lounging of their men. Occasionally a woman of high degree passes on a mule; under a vast felt hat her face is completely bandaged over with white silk, so that only the two eyes appear, like those of a hooded rider of the Ku Klux Klan. There are numerous priests, distinguished by long gowns and high turbans. Sometimes the emperor passes in a great red car surrounded by cantering lancers. A page sits behind holding over his head an umbrella of crimson silk embroidered with sequins and gold tassels. A guard sits in front nursing a machine-gun under a plush shawl; the chauffeur is a European wearing powder-blue livery and the star of Ethiopia.

There are open fields immediately round the station, broken on one side by the thin roof of the public baths, where a spring wells up scalding hot. It is from here that the water is conveyed in petrol-cans for our baths at the hotel. On the other side of the road stands the execution shed. Public hanging has recently been abolished in Tafari's own provinces, and the gibbet-tree before the cathedral cut down to make room for a little (unfinished) garden and a statue of Menelik. Homicides are now shot behind closed doors, though the bereaved relatives still retain the right of carrying out the sentence. No distinction is made in Abyssinian law between manslaughter and murder; both are treated as offences against the family of the dead man. It is for them to choose whether they will take blood-money or blood; the price varies with the social status of the deceased, but is usually about a thousand dollars (£70 or £80). Occasionally the murderer prefers to die rather than pay. There was a case in Addis Ababa shortly before our arrival in which the bargaining was continued in the execution shed right up to the firing of the shot; the relatives abating their price dollar by dollar, the murderer steadfastly refusing to deprive his children of their full inheritance.

As part of the general policy for tidying up the town

for the arrival of the visitors, high stockades have been erected, or are being erected, down all the streets, screening from possibly critical eyes the homes of the poorer inhabitants. Halfway up the hill stands the Hôtel de France, a place of primitive but cordial hospitality, kept by a young Frenchman and his wife who have seen better days as traders in hides and coffee at Djibouti. At the top of the hill, in front of the post office, two main roads branch out to right and left, the one leading to the Gebbi (Tafari's palace), the other to the native bazaar and Indian quarter. Work is in progress at the crossroads making a paved and balustraded island round a concrete cenotaph which is destined to commemorate the late empress. A fourth road leads obliquely to Gorgis, the cathedral of St George.

The buildings are mostly of concrete and corrugated iron. There is another large hotel kept by a Greek, the Imperial, most of which has been requisitioned for the Egyptian delegation. There are two or three small hotels, cafés, and bars, kept either by Greeks or Armenians. There is another large hotel under construction. It was being made specially for the coronation, but is still hopelessly unready. It is here that the Marine band of H.M.S. *Effingham* are put up. A night-club advertises that it will open shortly with a cabaret straight from the Winter Garden Theatre in Munich; it is called Haile Selassie (Power of the Trinity). This is the new name which the emperor has assumed among his other titles; a heavy fine is threatened to anyone overheard referring to him as Tafari. The words have become variously corrupted by the European visitors to 'Highly

Salacious' and 'I love a lassie' – this last the inspiration of a R.A.C. mechanic.

The bank and the manager's house are the two most solid buildings in the town; they stand behind a high wall in a side street between the two hotels. Round them are the two or three villas of the European traders, the bank officials, and the English chaplain. The shops are negligible; wretched tin stores, kept by Indians and Armenians, peddling tinned foods, lumps of coarse soap, and tarnished hardware. There is one shop of interest near the bank, kept by a French-speaking Abyssinian. It is called 'Curiosities' and exhibits anything from monkey-skins and cheap native jewellery to Amharic illuminated manuscripts of antiquity. Here I bought a number of modern Abyssinian paintings, mostly either hunting-scenes or intensely savage battle-pictures. Painting is more or less a hereditary craft in Abyssinia. It is in regular demand for ecclesiastical decoration. The churches of Abyssinia are all built on the same plan of a square inner sanctuary enclosed in two concentric ambulatories; sometimes the outside plan is octagonal, sometimes circular. It is very rarely that anyone except the priests is allowed to see into the sanctuary. Attention is concentrated on its walls, which are covered with frescos. The designs are traditional and are copied and recopied, generation after generation, with slight variation. When they begin to grow shabby and the church can afford it, a painter is called in to repaint them, as in Europe one calls in the paperhanger. In the intervals of executing these commissions the more skilful painters keep their hands in by doing secular work on sheets of linen or skins; these too are traditional in composition, but the artist is allowed more freedom in detail. His chief concern is to bring the old patterns up to date, and this he does, irrespective of historical propriety, by the introduction of topis, aeroplanes, and bombs. The secretary of the American Legation gave me a particularly delightful representation of the death of the Harar giant; this story is a very early medieval legend, probably connected with the wars against the Arabs, but the artist has drawn the giant-slayers with the khaki uniforms and fixed bayonets of Tafari's latest guard – a happy change after the stale, half-facetious, pre-Raphaelite archaism that seems ineradicable in English taste.

The Gebbi is a great jumble of buildings on a hill to the east of the town. At night, during coronation week, it was lit up with rows of electric bulbs, but by day it presented a slightly dingy appearance. The nucleus consists of a stone building containing a throne-room and banqueting-hall; a glazed corridor runs down one side, many of the panes were broken and all were dirty; the front is furnished with a double staircase and portico, clearly of classic sympathies. It was made for Menelik by a French architect. (It might well have been the hôtel de ville of some French provincial town.) In front of this is an untidy courtyard, irregular in shape, littered with loose stones and blown paper, and, all round it, sheds and outbuildings of all kinds and sizes; tin guard-houses, a pretty thatched chapel, barn-like apartments of various Court officials, servants' quarters, laundry and kitchens, a domed mausoleum in debased Byzantine style, a look-out tower and a barrack square. High walls encircle the whole, and the only approach, through which came alike butchers and ambassadors, is through two heavily guarded doors. In spite of this, the precincts seemed to be always full of loafers, squatting and squabbling, or gaping at the visitors.

The American Legation is not far from the centre of the town, but the British, French, and Italians all live beyond the racecourse, five or six miles out. Menelik chose the site of the concession, and the reason usually given for their remoteness is to ensure their safety in case of trouble. In point of fact, they are wholly indefensible, and, if an attack were ever made on them, would be unable to withstand half a day's siege. The social result, for better or worse, has been to divorce the diplomatic corps from the general life of the town. It may be this that Menelik desired.

It is now possible to reach the British Legation by car; until quite lately guests rode out to dinner on mules, a boy running in front with a lantern. Indeed, as further preparation for the visitors, the road from the town had been strewn with stones, and a motor-roller of the latest pattern brought from Europe; this machine was sometimes seen heading for the legations, but some untoward event always interposed, and the greater part of the way was left to be rolled by the tyres of private cars. It was an expensive and bumpy journey.

The legation stands in a small park with the consulate next to it, and on either side of the drive a little garden city has sprung up of pretty thatched bungalows which accommodate the other officials. During the coronation a camp was pitched in the paddock for the staffs of the various visitors, and periodic bugling, reminiscent of an ocean liner, added a fresh incongruity to the bizarre life of the little community. At normal times this consisted of the Minister, lately arrived from Shanghai, a Chinese scholar whose life's work had been in the Far East; the secretary, lately arrived from Constantinople; the consul, lately arrived from Fez, an authority and enthusiast in Mohammedan law (none of these had yet had time to learn any Amharic); the archivist, who had spent five or six years at Addis and knew how to mark out tennis-courts; the vice-consul, who performed prodigies of skill in sorting out luggage and looking up trains, despite the fact that he was all the time seriously ill from the after-effects of blackwater fever, and the oriental secretary, whom a perfect command of Amharic and fair smattering of English made invaluable as official interpreter.

Besides the officials and officers of all grades who now swelled the household, a substantial family party of uncles, aunts, and cousins had come out from England to see the fun. Housekeeping assumed a scale unprecedented in Addis Ababa, but all moved smoothly; a cook was specially imported from London who, happily enough, turned out to be named Mr Cook; the invitation cards from the British Legation greatly surpassed those of all other nations in thickness, area, and propriety of composition, and when it was discovered that by an engraver's error the name *Haile* had become *Hailu* (the name of the most formidable of the rival rases) no pains were spared to correct each card in pen and ink; the Duke's luggage was no sooner lost by one official than it was recovered by another.

Everything bore witness to the triumph of Anglo-Saxon organization.

Outside the legations was a personnel of supreme diversity. There was the Caucasian manager of the Haile Selassie Casino; the French editor of the *Courier d'Éthiope*, an infinitely helpful man, genial, punctilious, sceptical; an Englishman in the employ of the Abyssinian Government, debonair of appearance, but morbidly ill at ease in the presence of journalists before whom he might betray himself into some indiscretion; a French architect married to an Abyssinian; a bankrupt German planter obsessed by grievances; a tipsy old Australian prospector, winking over his whiskey and hinting at the mountains full of platinum he could tell you about if he cared to. There was Mr Hall, in whose office I spent many frantic hours; he was a trader, of mixed German and Abyssinian descent, extremely handsome, well dressed, and monocled, a man of imperturbable courtesy, an exceptional linguist. During the coronation he had been put in a little tin house next to the Casino and constituted chief, and, as far as one could see, sole member, of a *bureau d'étrangers*. It was his week's task to listen to all the troubles of all the foreigners, official or unofficial, to distribute news to the Press, issue tickets and make out lists for the Abyssinian functions; if the Italian telegraph company took an hour's rest, it was Mr Hall who heard the complaints; if an officious police-officer refused someone admittance to some grandstand, Mr Hall must see to it that the officer was reprimanded; if His Majesty's Stationery Office forgot to issue the text of the coronation service, Mr

Hall promised everyone a copy; if a charabanc had not arrived to take the band to the racecourse, if there had not been enough coronation medals to go round the church, if, for any reason or no reason, anyone in Addis Ababa was in a bad temper – and at that altitude the most equable natures become unaccountably upset – off he went to Mr Hall. And whatever language he cared to speak, Mr Hall would understand and sympathize; with almost feminine delicacy he would calm him and compliment him; with masculine decision he would make a bold note of the affair on his pad; he would rise, bow, and smile his pacified visitor out with every graceful assurance of goodwill – and do absolutely nothing about it.

Of the Abyssinians we saw very little except as grave, rather stolid figures at the official receptions. There was Ras Hailu, owner of the rich province of Gojam, reputed wealthier than the emperor himself; a commanding figure, dark complexioned, and his little pointed beard dyed black, and slightly insolent eyes. Among his many great possessions was a night-club two miles out on the Addis Alem road. He had planned this himself and, wishing to be up to date, had given it an English name. It was called 'Robinson'. There was the venerable Ras Kassa and Moulungetta, the commander-in-chief of the army, a mountain of a man with grey beard and bloodshot eyes; in full-dress uniform with scarlet-and-gold cloak and lion's mane busby, he looked hardly human; there was George Herui, son of the Minister of Foreign Affairs, the product of an English university – a slight young man dressed with great elegance either in

European clothes or in the uniform of a Court page; his father stood high in the emperor's confidence; George's interest, however, seemed mainly Parisian.

Apart from the officials and journalists who pullulated at every corner, there were surprisingly few visitors. At one time Messrs Thomas Cook & Company were advertising a personally conducted tour, an announcement which took a great deal of the romance out of our expedition. The response was considerable, but when their agent arrived it soon became apparent that the enterprise was impracticable; there was no certainty of transport or accommodation, and, with soaring prices and fluctuating currency, it was impossible to give an estimate of the expenses involved. So the tour was cancelled, but the agent remained, a cocksure, dapper little Italian, an unfailing source of inaccurate information on all local topics.

There was a slightly class-conscious lady with a French title and an American accent, who left the town suddenly after a luncheon-party at which she was not accorded her proper precedence. There was the American professor, who will appear later in this narrative, and two formidable ladies in knitted suits and topis; though unrelated by blood, long companionship had made them almost indistinguishable, square-jawed, tight-lipped, with hard, discontented eyes. For them the whole coronation was a profound disappointment. What did it matter that they were witnesses of a unique stage of the interpenetration of two cultures? They were out for Vice. They were collecting material, in fact, for a little book on the subject, an African *Mother India*, and every minute devoted to Coptic ritual or displays of horsemanship was a minute wasted. Prostitution and drug traffic comprised their modest interests, and they were too dense to find evidence of either.

But perhaps the most remarkable visitors were the Marine band. At first the emperor had intended to import a European dance-band from Cairo, but the estimate for fees and expenses was so discouraging that he decided instead to issue an invitation to the band of H.M.S. *Effingham* to attend the coronation as his guests and to play at the various functions. They arrived on the same day as the Duke of Gloucester, under the command of Major Sinclair, strengthened by a diet of champagne at breakfast, luncheon, tea, and dinner throughout their journey, and much sage advice about the propriety of their behaviour in a foreign capital. At Addis they were quartered in a large, unfinished hotel; each man had his own bedroom, furnished by his thoughtful hosts with hairbrushes, clothes-hangers, and brand-new enamelled spittoons.

Perhaps no one did more to deserve his star of Ethiopia than Major Sinclair. Eschewing the glitter and dignity of the legation camp, he loyally remained with his men in the town, and spent anxious days arranging appointments that were never kept; his diary, which some of us were privileged to see, was a stark chronicle of successive disappointments patiently endured. 'Appointment 9.30 emperor's private secretary to arrange for this evening's banquet; he did not come. 11. Went as arranged to see master of the king's music; he was not there. 12. Went to see Mr Hall to obtain score of Ethiopian national anthem

– not procurable. 2.30. Car should have come to take men to aerodrome – did not arrive . . .' and so on. But, in spite of every discouragement, the band was always present on time, irreproachably dressed, and provided with the correct music.

One morning in particular, on which the band played a conspicuous part, remains vividly in my memory as typical of the whole week. It was the first day of the official celebrations, to be inaugurated by the unveiling of the new Menelik memorial. The ceremony was announced for ten o'clock. Half an hour before the time, Irene Ravensdale and I drove to the spot. Here, on the site of the old execution-tree, stood the monument, shrouded in brilliant green silk. Round it was a little ornamental garden with paving, a balustrade, and regular plots, from which, here and there, emerged delicate shoots of newly sown grass. While some workmen were laying carpets on the terrace and spreading yellow sunshades of the kind which cover the tables at open-air restaurants, others were still chipping at the surrounding masonry and planting drooping palm-trees in the arid beds. A heap of gilt armchairs lay on one side; on the other a mob of photographers and movietone men were fighting for places. Opposite the carpeted terrace rose a stand of several unstable tiers. A detachment of policemen were engaged furiously laying about them with canes in the attempt to keep these seats clear of natives. Four or five Europeans were already established there. Irene and I joined them. Every ten minutes or so a police officer would appear and order us all off; we produced our *laissez-passers*; he saluted and went away, to be succeeded at a short interval by a colleague, when the performance was repeated.

The square and half a mile of the avenue approaching it were lined with royal guards; there was a band formed up in front of them; the Belgian colonel curvetted about on an uneasy chestnut horse. Presently, punctual to the minute, appeared Major Sinclair and his band. They had had to march from their hotel, as the charabanc ordered for them had failed to appear. They halted, and Major Sinclair approached the Belgian colonel for instructions. The colonel knew no English, and the major no French; an embarrassing interview followed, complicated by the caprices of the horse, which plunged backwards and sideways over the square. In this way the two officers covered a large area of ground, conversing inconclusively the while with extravagant gestures. Eventually Irene heroically stepped out to interpret for them. It appeared that the Belgian colonel had had no orders about the English band. He had his own band there and did not want another. The major explained he had had direct instructions to appear in the square at ten. The colonel said the major could not possibly stay in the square; there was no room for him, and anyway he would have no opportunity of playing, since the native band had a programme of music fully adequate for the whole proceedings. (Knowing that band's tendency to repetition, we could well believe it.) At last the colonel conceded that the English band might take up a position at the extreme end of his troops at the bottom of the hill. The officers parted, and the band marched away out of sight. A long wait followed, while the battle between police and populace raged round the stand. At last the delegations began to arrive; the soldiers presented arms; the native band played the appropriate music; the Belgian colonel was borne momentarily backwards through the ranks, capered heroically among the crowd, and reappeared at another corner of the square. The delegations took up their places on the gilt chairs under the umbrellas. A long pause preceded the emperor's arrival; the soldiers still stood stiff. Suddenly up that imposing avenue there appeared a slave, trotting unconcernedly with a gilt chair on his head. He put it among the others, looked round with interest at the glittering uniforms, and then retired. At last the emperor came; first a troop of lancers, then the crimson car and silk umbrella. He took up his place in the centre of the Court under a blue canopy; the band played the Ethiopian national anthem. A secretary presented him with the text of his speech; the cameramen began snapping and turning. But there was a fresh delay. Something had gone wrong. Messages passed from mouth to mouth; a runner disappeared down the hill.

One photographer, bolder than the rest, advanced out of the crowd and planted his camera within a few yards of the royal party; he wore a violet suit of plusfours, a green shirt open at the neck, tartan stockings, and parti-coloured shoes. After a few happy shots of the emperor he walked slowly along the line, looking the party critically up and down. When he found anyone who attracted his attention, he took a photograph of him. Then, expressing his satisfaction with a slight inclination of the head, he rejoined his colleagues.

Still a delay. Then up the avenue came Major Sinclair and the Marine band. They halted in the middle of the square, arranged their music, and played the national anthem. Things were then allowed to proceed according to plan. The emperor advanced, read his speech, and pulled the cord. There was a rending of silk and a vast equestrian figure in gilt bronze was partially revealed. Men appeared with poles and poked away the clinging folds. One piece, out of reach of their efforts, obstinately fluttered over the horse's ears and eyes. The Greek contractor mounted a ladder and dislodged the rag.

The Marine band continued to play; the delegations and courtiers made for their cars; the emperor paused, and listened attentively to the music, then smiled his approval to the major before driving away. As the last of the visitors disappeared, the people broke through the soldiers, and the square became a dazzle of white tunics and black heads. For many days to come, numbers of them might be seen clustering round the memorial and gazing with puzzled awe at this new ornament to their city.

Until late on the preceding afternoon, wild uncertainty prevailed about the allocation of tickets for the coronation. The legations knew nothing. Mr Hall knew nothing, and his office was continuously besieged by anxious journalists whose only hope of getting their reports back in time for Monday's papers was to write and dispatch them well before the event. What could they say when they did not even know where the ceremony would take place?

With little-disguised irritation they set to work making the best of their meagre material. Gorgis and its precincts were impenetrably closed; a huge tent could be discerned through the railings, built against one wall of the church. Some described the actual coronation as taking place there; others used it as the scene of a state reception and drew fanciful pictures of the ceremony in the interior of the cathedral, *'murky, almost suffocating with incense and the thick, stifling smoke of tallow candles'* (Associated Press); authorities on Coptic ritual remarked that as the coronation proper must take place in the inner sanctuary, which no layman might glimpse, much less enter, there was small hope of anyone seeing anything at all, unless, conceivably, exceptions were made of the Duke of Gloucester and Prince Udine. The cinema-men, whose companies had spent very large sums in importing them and their talking apparatus, began to show signs of restlessness, and some correspondents became almost menacing in their representations of the fury of a slighted Press. Mr Hall, however, remained his own serene self. Everything, he assured us, was being arranged for our particular convenience; only, he admitted, the exact details were still unsettled.

Eventually, about fourteen hours before the ceremony was due to start, numbered tickets were issued through the legations; there was plenty of room for all, except, as it happened, for the Abyssinians themselves. The rases and Court officials were provided with gilt chairs, but the local chiefs seemed to be wholly neglected; most of them remained outside, gazing wistfully at the ex-Kaiser's coach and the tall hats of the

European and American visitors; those that succeeded in pushing their way inside were kept far at the back, where they squatted together on their haunches, or, in all the magnificent trappings of their gala dress, dozed simply in distant corners of the great tent.

For it was there, in the end, that the service took place. 'Tent', however, gives an incomplete impression of this fine pavilion. It was light and lofty, supported by two colonnades of draped scaffold-poles; the east end was hung with silk curtains, behind which a sanctuary had been improvised to hold the tabor from the cathedral. A carpeted dais ran half the length of the floor. On it stood the silk-covered table that bore the regalia and the crown neatly concealed in a cardboard hat-box; on either side were double rows of gilt chairs for the Court and the diplomatic corps, and at the end, with their backs to the body of the hall, two canopied thrones, one scarlet for the emperor and one blue for the empress.

Their Majesties had spent the night in vigil, surrounded inside the cathedral by clergy, and outside by troops; when they entered the tent it was from behind the curtains by means of a side door leading directly from the cathedral. One enterprising journalist headed his report '*Meditation Behind Machine-Guns*', and had the gratifying experience when he was at last admitted into the precincts, of finding his guess fully justified; a machine section was posted on the steps covering each approach. Other predictions were less happy. Many correspondents, for instance, wrote accounts of the emperor's solemn progress from the palace at sundown; actually it was late at night before he arrived, and then with the minimum of display. The Associated Press postponed the event until dawn, and described it in these terms: *'As their Majesties rode to church through the dusty streets of the mountain capital, which were packed with tens of thousands of their braves and chieftains, the masses uttered savage cries of acclaim. Scores of natives were trampled in the dust as the crowd surged to catch sight of the coronation party.'*

It was highly interesting to me, when the papers began to arrive from Europe and America, to compare my own experiences with those of the different correspondents. I had the fortune to be working for a paper which values the accuracy of its news before everything else; even so I was betrayed into a few mistakes. Telegraphic economy accounts for some of these, as when 'Abuna', the title of the Abyssinian primate, became expanded by a zealous sub-editor into 'the Archbishop of Abuna'. Proper names often came through somewhat mangled, and curious transpositions of whole phrases occasionally took place, so that somewhere between Addis Ababa and London I was saddled with the amazing assertion that George Herui had served on Sir John Maffey's staff in the Soudan. Some mistakes of this kind seem inevitable. My surprise in reading the Press reports of the coronation was not that my more impetuous colleagues had allowed themselves to be slapdash about their details or that they had fallen into some occasional exaggeration of the more romantic and incongruous aspects of the affair. It seemed to me that we had been witnesses of a quite different series of events. 'Getting in first with the news' and 'giving the public what it wants', the two dominating principles of Fleet Street, are not always reconcilable.

I do not intend by this any conventional condemnation of the 'Yellow Press'. It seems to me that a prig is someone who judges people by his own, rather than by their, standards; criticism only becomes useful when it can show people where their own principles are in conflict. It is perfectly natural that the cheaper newspapers should aim at entertainment rather than instruction, and give prominence to what is startling and frivolous over what is important but unamusing or unintelligible. 'If a dog bites a man, that's nothing; if a man bites a dog, that's news.' My complaint is that in its scramble for precedence the cheap Press is falling short of the very standards of public service it has set itself. Almost any London newspaper, today, would prefer an incomplete, inaccurate, and insignificant report of an event provided it came in time for an earlier edition than its rivals. Now the public is not concerned with this competition. The reader, opening his paper on the breakfast-table, has no vital interest in, for instance, Abyssinian affairs. An aeroplane accident or boxing-match are a different matter. In these cases he simply wants to know the result as soon as possible. But the coronation of an African emperor means little or nothing to him. He may read about it on Monday or Tuesday, he will not be impatient. All he wants from Africa is something to amuse him in the railway train to his office. He will be just as much amused on Tuesday as on Monday. The extra day's delay makes the difference, to the correspondent on the spot, of whether he has time to compose a fully informed account (and, in almost all cases, the better informed the account the more entertaining it will be to the reader). Or at least it makes this difference. Events in a newspaper become amusing and thrilling just in so far as they are given credence as historical facts. Anyone, sitting down for a few hours with a typewriter, could compose a paper that would be the ideal of every news-editor. He would deal out dramatic deaths in the royal family, derail trains, embroil the country in civil war, and devise savage and insoluble murders. All these things would be profoundly exciting to the reader so long as he thought they were true. If they were offered to him as fiction they would be utterly insignificant. (And this shows the great gulf which divides the novelist from the journalist. The value of a novel depends on the standards each book evolves for itself; incidents which have no value as news are given any degree of importance according to their place in the book's structure and their relation to other incidents in the composition, just as subdued colours attain great intensity in certain pictures.) The delight of reading the popular newspapers does not come, except quite indirectly, from their political programmes or 'feature articles', but from the fitful illumination which glows in odd places – phrases reported from the police courts, statements made in public orations in provincial towns – which suddenly reveal unexpected byways of life. If these were pure invention they would lose all interest. As soon as one knows that they are written with conscious satire by some bright young reporter in the office, there is no further amusement in the astounding opinions so dogmatically expressed in the correspondence column.

In Addis Ababa, for the first time, I was able to watch the machinery of journalism working in a simplified form. A London office is too full and complicated to enable one to form opinions on any brief acquaintance. Here I knew most of the facts and people involved, and in the light of this knowledge I found the Press reports shocking and depressing. After all, there really was something there to report that was quite new to the European public; a succession of events of startling spectacular character, and a system of life, in a tangle of modernism and barbarity, European, African, and American, of definite, individual character. It seemed to me that here, at least, the truth was stranger than the newspaper reports. For instance, one newspaper stated that the emperor's banqueting-hall was decorated with inlaid marble, ivory, and malachite. That is not very strange to anyone who has been into any of the cheaper London hotels. In actual fact there were photographs of Mr Ramsay MacDonald and M. Poincaré, and a large, very lifelike oil-painting of a lion, by an Australian artist. It all depends on what one finds amusing. In the same way the royal coach was reported to have been drawn from the church by six milk-white horses – a wholly banal conception of splendour. If the reporters had wanted to say something thrilling, why did they not say gilded eunuchs, or ostriches with dyed plumes, or a team of captive kings, blinded and wearing yokes of elephant tusk? But since custom or poverty of imagination confined them to the stables, why should they not content themselves with what actually happened, that the ex-Kaiser's coach appeared at the church equipped with six horses (they were not white, but that is immaterial) and a Hungarian coachman in fantastic circus livery, but that, as they had never been properly trained, they proved difficult to manage and at the first salute of guns fell into utter confusion, threatening destruction to the coach and causing grave alarm to the surrounding crowds; that finally two had to be unharnessed, and that this was not accomplished until one groom had been seriously injured; that next day in the procession the coachman did not appear, and the emperor resumed his crimson motor-car – a triumph of modernism typical of the whole situation?

This is what I saw at the coronation:

The emperor and empress were due to appear from their vigil at seven in the morning. We were warned to arrive at the tent about an hour before that time. Accordingly, having dressed by candlelight, Irene and I proceeded there at about six. For many hours before dawn the roads into the town had been filled with tribesmen coming in from the surrounding camps. We could see them passing the hotel (the street lamps were working that night) in dense white crowds, some riding mules, some walking, some moving at a slow trot beside their masters. All, as always, were armed. Our car moved slowly to Gorgis, hooting continuously. There were many other cars; some carrying Europeans; others, Abyssinian officials. Eventually we reached the church and were admitted after a narrow scrutiny of our tickets and ourselves. The square inside the gates was comparatively clear; from the top of the steps the machine-guns compromised with ecclesiastical calm. From inside the cathedral came the voices of the priests singing the last phase of the service that had lasted all night. Eluding the numerous soldiers, policemen, and officials who directed us towards the tent, we slipped into the outer ambulatory of the church, where the choir of bearded and vested deacons were dancing to the music of hand drums and little silver rattles. The drummers squatted round them; but they carried the rattles themselves and in their other hand waved praying-sticks.* Some carried nothing, but merely clapped their empty palms. They shuffled in and out, singing and swaying; the dance was performed with body and arms rather than with the feet. Their faces expressed the keenest enjoyment – almost, in some cases, ecstasy. The brilliant morning sun streamed in on them from the windows, on their silver crosses, silver-headed rods, and on the large, illu- minated manuscript from which one of them, un- deterred by the music, was reciting the Gospels; the clouds of incense mounted and bellied in the shafts of light.

Presently we went on to the tent. This was already well filled. The clothes of the congregation varied considerably. Most of the men were wearing morning coats, but some had appeared in evening dress and one or two in dinner-jackets. One lady had stuck an American flag in the top of her sun-helmet. The junior members of the legations were there already, in

* These are long rods with crooked handles; the Abyssinians prostrate themselves frequently, but do not kneel in prayer; instead, they stand resting their hands on the stick and their forehead on their hands.

uniform, fussing among the seats to see that everything was in order. By seven o'clock the delegations arrived. The English party, led by the Duke of Gloucester and Lord Airlie in hussar and lancer uniforms, were undoubtedly the most august, though there was a very smart Swede carrying a silver helmet. It happened that our delegation was largely composed of men of unusually imposing physique; it was gratifying both to our own national loyalty (an emotion which becomes surprisingly sensible in remote places) and also to that of the simpler Abyssinians, who supposed, rightly enough, that this magnificent array was there with the unequivocal purpose of courtesy towards the emperor; I am rather more doubtful, however, about the impression made on the less uneducated classes. They have deep suspicions of the intentions of their European neighbours, and the parade of our own war lords (as Sir John Maffey, Sir Harold Kittermaster, Sir Stewart Symes, Admiral Fullerton, and Mr Noble, in full uniform, may well have appeared in their eyes) was little calculated to allay them. It is perhaps significant to note that important commercial contracts and advisory positions at Court have recently been accorded to the least demonstrative of the visiting nations – the United States of America. However, it is churlish to complain that our public servants are too handsome, and, as far as the coronation ceremonies went, they certainly added glamour to the pageant.

It was long after the last delegate had taken his place that the emperor and empress appeared from the church. We could hear the singing going on behind the curtains.

Photographers, amateur and professional, employed the time in taking furtive snapshots. Reporters dispatched their boys to the telegraph office with supplementary accounts of the preliminaries. By some misunderstanding of the instructions of the responsible official, the office was closed for the day. After the manner of native servants, the messengers, instead of reporting the matter to their masters, sat, grateful for the rest, on the steps gossiping until it should open. It was late in the day that the truth became known, and then there was more trouble for Mr Hall.

The ceremony was immensely long, even according to the original schedule, and the clergy succeeded in prolonging it by at least an hour and a half beyond the allotted time. The six succeeding days of celebration were to be predominantly military, but the coronation day itself was in the hands of the Church, and they were going to make the most of it. Psalms, canticles, and prayers succeeded each other, long passages of Scripture were read, all in the extinct ecclesiastical tongue, Ghiz. Candles were lit one by one; the coronation oaths were proposed and sworn; the diplomats shifted uncomfortably in their gilt chairs, noisy squabbles broke out round the entrance between the imperial guard and the retainers of the local chiefs. Professor W., who was an expert of high transatlantic reputation on Coptic ritual, occasionally remarked: 'They are beginning the Mass now,' 'That was the offertory,' 'No, I was wrong; it was the consecration,' 'No, I was wrong; I think it is the secret Gospel,' 'No, I think it must be the Epistle,' 'How very curious; I don't believe it was a Mass at all,' '*Now* they *are* beginning the Mass . . .' and so on. Presently the bishops began to fumble among the bandboxes, and investiture began. At long intervals the emperor was presented with robe, orb, spurs, spear, and finally with the crown. A salute of guns was fired, and the crowds outside, scattered all over the surrounding waste spaces, began to cheer; the imperial horses reared up, plunged on top of each other, kicked the gilding off the front of the coach, and broke their traces. The coachman sprang from the box and whipped them from a safe distance. Inside the pavilion there was a general sense of relief; it had all been very fine and impressive, now for a cigarette, a drink, and a change into less formal costume. Not a bit of it. The next thing was to crown the empress and the heir apparent; another salvo of guns followed, during which an Abyssinian groom had two ribs broken in an attempt to unharness a pair of the imperial horses. Again we felt for our hats and gloves. But the Coptic choir still sang; the bishops then proceeded to take back the regalia with proper prayers, lections, and canticles.

'I have noticed some very curious variations in the Canon of the Mass,' remarked the professor, 'particularly with regard to the kiss of peace.'

Then the Mass began.

For the first time throughout the morning the emperor and empress left their thrones; they disappeared behind the curtains into the improvised sanctuary; most of the clergy went too. The stage was empty save for the diplomats; their faces were set and strained, their attitudes inelegant. I have seen just that look in crowded second-class railway carriages, at dawn, between Avignon and Marseille. Their clothes made them funnier still. Marshal d'Esperez alone preserved his dignity, his chest thrown out, his baton poised on his knee, rigid as a war memorial, and, as far as one could judge, wide awake.

It was now about eleven o'clock, the time at which the emperor was due to leave the pavilion. Punctually to plan, three Abyssinian aeroplanes rose to greet him. They circled round and round over the tent, eagerly demonstrating their newly acquired art by swooping and curvetting within a few feet of the canvas roof. The noise was appalling; the local chiefs stirred in their sleep and rolled on to their faces; only by the opening and closing of their lips and the turning of their music could we discern that the Coptic deacons were still singing.

'A most unfortunate interruption. I missed many of the verses,' said the professor.

Eventually, at about half-past twelve, the Mass came to an end, and the emperor and empress, crowned, shuffling along under a red and gold canopy, and looking as Irene remarked, exactly like the processional statues of Seville, crossed to a grandstand, from which the emperor delivered a royal proclamation; an aeroplane scattered copies of the text and, through loudspeakers, the Court heralds reread it to the populace.

There was a slightly ill-tempered scramble among the photographers and cinema-men – I received a heavy blow in the middle of the back from a large camera, and a hoarse rebuke. 'Come along there now – let the eyes of the world see.'

Dancing broke out once more among the clergy, and there is no knowing how long things might not have gone on, had not the photographers so embarrassed and jostled them, and outraged their sense of reverence, that they withdrew to finish their devotions alone in the cathedral.

Then at last the emperor and empress were conducted to their coach and borne off to luncheon by its depleted but still demonstratively neurasthenic team of horses.

Having finished the report for my paper, which I had been composing during the service, I delivered it to the wireless operator at the Italian Legation; as I began to search for my car the Belgian major rose up and began insulting me; I could not quite understand why until I learned that he mistook me for a German bank-clerk who apparently had lately boxed the ears of his orderly. My Indian chauffeur had got bored and gone home. Luncheon at the hotel was odious. All food supplies had been commandeered by the Government, M. Hallot told us; it was rather doubtful whether the market would open again until the end of the week. Meanwhile there were tinned chunks of pineapple and three courses of salt beef, one cut in small cubes with chopped onion, one left in a slab with tomato ketchup, one in slices with hot water and Worcestershire sauce; the waiters had gone out the night before to get drunk and had not yet woken up.

We were all in a bad temper that night.

Six days followed of intensive celebration. On Monday morning the delegations were required to leave wreaths at the mausoleum of Menelik and Zauditu. This is a circular, domed building of vaguely Byzantine affinities, standing in the Gebbi grounds. Its interior is furnished with oil-paintings and enlarged photographs of the royal family, a fumed oak grandfather clock, and a few occasional tables of the kind exhibited in shop windows in Tottenham Court Road; their splay legs protruded from under embroidered linen tablecloths, laid diagonally; on them stood little conical silver vases of catkins boldly counterfeited in wire and magenta wool. Steps led down to the vault where lay the white marble sarcophagi of the two potentates. It is uncertain whether either contains the body attributed to it, or indeed any body at all. The date and place of Menelik's death are a palace secret, but it is generally supposed to have taken place about two years before its formal announcement to people; the empress probably lies out under the hill at Debra Lebanos. At various hours that morning, however, the delegations of the Great Powers dutifully appeared with fine bundles of flowers, and, not to be outdone in reverence, Professor W. came tripping gravely in with a little bunch of white carnations.

There was a cheerful, friendly tea-party that afternoon at the American Legation and a ball and firework display at the Italian, but the party which excited the keenest interest was the *gebbur* given by the emperor to his tribesmen. These banquets are a regular feature of Ethiopian life, constituting, in fact, a vital bond between the people and their overlords, whose prestige in time of peace varied directly with their frequency and abundance. Until a few years ago attendance at a *gebbur* was part of the entertainment offered to every visitor in Abyssinia. Copious first-hand accounts can be found in almost every book about the country, describing the packed, squatting ranks of the diners; the slaves carrying the warm quarters of newly slaughtered, uncooked beef; the dispatch with which each guest carves for himself; the upward slice of his dagger with which he severs each mouthful from the dripping lump; the flat, damp platters of local bread; the great draughts of *tedj* and *talla* from the horn drinking-pots; the butchers outside felling and dividing the oxen; the emperor and notables at the high table, exchanging highly seasoned morsels of more elaborate fare. These are the traditional features of the *gebbur* and, no doubt, of this occasion also. It was thus that the journalists described their impressions in glowing paraphrases of Rhey and Kingsford. When the time came, however, we found that particular precautions had been taken to exclude all Europeans from the spectacle. Perhaps it was felt that the feast might give a false impression of the civilizing pretensions of the Government. Mr Hall loyally undertook to exercise his influence for each of us personally, but in the end no one gained admission except two resolute ladies and, by what was felt to be a very base exploitation of racial advantage, the coloured correspondent of a syndicate of Negro newspapers.

All that I saw was the last relay of guests shambling out of the Gebbi gates late that afternoon. They were a very enviable company, quite stupefied with food and drink. Policemen attempted to herd them on, kicking their insensible backs and whacking them with canes, but nothing disturbed their serene good temper. The chiefs were hoisted on to mules by their retainers and remained there blinking and smiling; one very old man, mounted back to front, felt feebly about the crupper for his reins; some stood clasped together in silent, swaying groups; others, lacking support, rolled contentedly in the dust. I remembered them that evening as I sat in the supper-room at the Italian Legation gravely discussing the slight disturbance of diplomatic propriety caused by the emperor's capricious distribution of honours.

There were several parties that week, of more or less identical composition. At three there were fireworks, resulting in at least one nasty accident; at one, a cinema which failed to work; at one, Gilla dancers who seemed to dislocate their shoulders, and sweated so heartily that our host was able to plaster their foreheads with banknotes; at another, Somali dancers shivered with cold on a lawn illuminated with coloured flares. There was a race meeting, where the local ponies plunged over low jumps and native jockeys cut off corners; the emperor sat all alone under a great canopy; the royal enclosure was packed and the rest of the course empty of spectators; a totalizator paid out four dollars on every winning three-dollar ticket; both bands played; Prince Udine presented an enormous cup and the emperor a magnificent kind of urn whose purpose no one could discover; it had several silver taps and little silver stands, and a great tray covered with silver cups of the kind from which grape-fruit is eaten in cinema-films. This fine trophy was won by a gentleman, in gilt riding-boots,

attached to the French Legation, and was used later at
their party for champagne. There was a certain amount
of whispering against French sportsmanship, however,
as they had sent back their books of sweepstake tickets
with scarcely one sold. This showed a very bad club
spirit, the other legations maintained.

There was a procession of all the troops, uniformed
and irregular, in the middle of which Irene appeared
in a taxicab surprisingly surrounded by a band of
mounted musicians playing six-foot pipes and banging
on saddle drums of oxhide and wood. The people all
shrilled their applause, as the emperor passed, in a high,
wailing whistle.

There was the opening of a museum of souvenirs,
containing examples of native craftsmanship, the crown
captured by General Napier at Magdala and returned
by the Victoria and Albert Museum, and a huge, hollow
stone which an Abyssinian saint had worn as a hat.

There was a review of the troops on the plain outside
the railway station. Although we had been privileged to
see almost every member of His Majesty's forces almost
every day, this was a startling display for those, like
myself, who had never seen a muster of tribesmen in
Arabia or Morocco. The men converged on the royal
stand from all over the plain, saluting him with cries
and flourishes of arms, the little horses and mules
galloping right up to the foot of the throne and being
reined back savagely on to their haunches, with mouths
dripping foam and blood.

But no catalogue of events can convey any real idea
of these astounding days, of an atmosphere utterly

unique, elusive, unforgettable. If in the foregoing pages I have seemed to give undue emphasis to the irregularity of the proceedings, to their unpunctuality, and their occasional failure, it is because this was an essential part of their character and charm. In Addis Ababa everything was haphazard and incongruous; one learned always to expect the unusual and yet was always surprised.

Every morning we awoke to a day of brilliant summer sunshine; every evening fell cool, limpid, charged with hidden vitality, fragrant with the thin smoke of the *tukal* fires, pulsing, like a live body, with the beat of the tom-toms that drummed incessantly somewhere out of sight among the eucalyptus-trees. In this rich African setting were jumbled together, for a few days, people of every race and temper, all involved in one way or another in that complex of hysteria and apathy, majesty and farce; a company shot through with every degree of animosity and suspicion. There were continual rumours born of the general uncertainty; rumours about the date and place of every ceremony; rumours of dissension in high places; rumours that, in the absence at Addis Ababa of all the responsible officials, the interior was seething with brigandage; rumours that Sir Percival Phillips had used the legation wireless; that the Ethiopian Minister to Paris had been refused admittance to Addis Ababa; that the royal coachman had not had his wages for two months and had given in his notice; that the airmen from Aden were secretly prospecting for a service between the capital and the coast; that one of the legations had refused to receive the empress's first lady-in-waiting;

above all, there was the great Flea Scandal and the Indiscretion about the Duke of Gloucester's Cook.

I had an intimation of that affair some days before it was generally known. Two journalists were drinking cocktails with me on the hotel terrace on the evening before the coronation. One of them said, 'We got a jolly good story this morning out of –,' naming an amiable nitwit on the Duke of Gloucester's staff. 'It isn't in your paper's line, so I don't mind telling you.'

The story was plain and credible; first, that the old Gebbi in which His Royal Highness was quartered was, like most houses in Ethiopia, infested with fleas; secondly that the German cook was unable to obtain due attention from the native servants and came to complain of the fact. She paced up and down the room passionately, explaining her difficulties; when she turned her back it was apparent that in her agitation she had failed to fasten her skirt, which fell open and revealed underclothes of red flannel; the English party were unable to hide their amusement, and the cook, thinking that the ridicule was part of a scheme of persecution, stormed out of the house, leaving the party without their breakfast.

'You sent that back?' I asked.

'You bet your life I did.'

I felt there might be trouble.

Two days later the local correspondent of one of the news agencies received the following message from London: *Investigate report fleas Gloucester's bed also cook red drawers left Duke breakfastless.'* He hurried with this cable to the legation and, on the Minister's advice cabled back, '*Insignificant incident greatly exaggerated advisable suppress.*'

But it was too late. The papers of the civilized world had published the story. The emperor's European agents had cabled back news of the betrayal; the emperor had complained to the legations. Stirring reports were in circulation that the emperor required every journalist to leave the country, bag and baggage, within twenty-four hours; that Lady Barton was revising her dance list; that the kantaba had cancelled his banquet; that no more stars of Ethiopia were to be dealt out until the culprit was discovered. Phrases such as 'breach of hospitality', 'gross ill-breeding', 'unpardonable irregularity', 'damned bad form' volleyed and echoed on every side. At a party that evening the A.D.C. who had caused the trouble was conspicuously vigorous in his aspirations to 'kick the bounder's backside, whoever he is'. We all felt uneasy for nearly a day, until the topic was succeeded by the French Legation's shabby behaviour over the sweepstake tickets, and the grave question of whether the emperor would attend Marshal d'Esperez's private tea-party.

One morning, a few days later, Irene and I were sitting outside the hotel drinking apéritifs and waiting for luncheon; we were entertained by the way in which the various visitors treated a pedlar who diffidently approached them with a bundle of bootlaces in one hand and an enamelled *pot de chambre* in the other. Suddenly a taxi drove up, and a servant wearing the palace livery jumped out and emptied a large pile of envelopes into Irene's lap. Two were addressed to us. We took them and handed back the rest, which the man presented, to be sorted in the same way, at the next table. It was not perhaps the most expeditious method of delivery, but, as he was unable to read, it is difficult to think of what else he could have done.

The envelopes contained an invitation to lunch with the emperor that day at one o'clock; as it was then after half-past twelve we disregarded the request for an answer and hurried off to change.

Professor W. had spoken to me of this party some days before, saying with restrained relish, 'On Saturday I am lunching with the emperor. There are several things I shall be interested to discuss with him.' But, as it turned out, he had little opportunity for conversation. There were about eighty guests and many empty places, showing that the messenger had not been able to finish his round in time (indeed, it is no unusual thing in Addis Ababa to receive cards of invitation many hours after the event). They were the European officials in the Abyssinian Government, European residents, journalists, and private visitors whose names had been sent in by the legations; the European officers of the army, a few Abyssinian notables, the wives of visiting consuls, and so on. At first we stood in the glazed corridor which ran down one side of the main building. Then we were ushered into the throne-room, bowed and curtsied, and ranged ourselves round the walls while *byrrh* and vermouth and cigars were carried round. There was something slightly ecclesiastical in the atmosphere.

The emperor then led the way into the dining-room. We tramped in behind him in no particular order. He seated himself at the centre of the top table; three tables ran at right angles to him, resplendent with gold plate and white-and-gold china. Typewritten name-cards lay on each plate. Ten minutes or so followed of some confusion as we jostled round and round looking for our places; there was no plan of the table, and as most of us were complete strangers we were unable to help each other. The emperor sat watching us with a placid little smile. We must have looked very amusing. Naturally no one cared to look at the places next to the emperor, so that when at last we were all seated the two most honoured guests were left to sidle forlornly into the nearest empty places. Eventually they were fetched. Irene sat on one side and the French wife of the Egyptian consul on his other. I sat between an English airman and a Belgian photographer. A long meal followed, of many courses of fair French cooking and good European wines. There was also *tedj* and the national beverage made from fermented honey. We had sent out for some, one evening at the hotel, and found it an opaque yellowish liquid, mild and rather characterless. The emperor's *tedj* was a very different drink, quite clear, slightly brown, heavy, rich, and dry. After luncheon, at Irene's request, we were given some of the liqueur distilled from it – a colourless spirit of fine flavour and disconcerting potency.

Only one odd thing happened at luncheon. Just as we were finishing, a stout young woman rose from a seat near the back and made her way resolutely between the tables until she planted herself within a few yards of the emperor. I understand that she was a Syrian Jewess employed in some educational capacity in the town. She carried a sheaf of papers which she held close to her pince-nez with one plump hand while she raised the other above her head in a Fascist salute. Conversation faltered and ceased. The emperor looked at her with kindly inquiry. Then, in a voice of peculiar strength and stridency, she began to recite an ode. It was a very long complimentary ode, composed by herself in Arabic, a language wholly unintelligible to His Majesty. Between verses she made a long pause during which she fluttered her manuscript; then she began again. We had just begun to feel that the performance would really prove interminable, when, just as suddenly as she had begun, she stopped, bobbed, turned about, and, with glistening forehead and slightly labouring breath, strode back to her place to receive the congratulations of her immediate neighbours. The emperor rose and led the way back to the throne-room. Here we stood round the walls for a quarter of an hour while liqueurs were served. Then we bowed in turn and filed out into the sunshine.

That evening at the hotel two soldiers appeared with a huge basket of coloured Harari work for Irene from the emperor. In it was a fine outfit of native woman's clothing, consisting of a pair of black satin trousers of great girth, an embroidered cloak, a hand woven *chamma*, and a set of gold ornaments.

One moment of that week is particularly vivid in my memory. It was late at night and we had just returned from a party. My room, as I have said, was in an outhouse at a little distance from the hotel; a grey horse, some goats, and the hotel guard, his head wrapped in a blanket, were sleeping in the yard as I went across.

Behind my room, separated from the hotel grounds by wooden palings, lay a cluster of native *tukals*. That evening there was a party in one of them – probably celebrating a wedding or funeral. The door faced my way and I could see a glimmer of lamplight in the interior. They were singing a monotonous song, clapping in time and drumming with their hands on petrol-tins. I suppose there were about ten or fifteen of them there. I stood for some time listening. I was wearing a tall hat, evening clothes and white gloves. Presently the guard woke up and blew a little trumpet; the sound was taken up by other guards at neighbouring houses (it is in this way that they assure their employers of their vigilance); then he wrapped himself once more in his blanket and relapsed into sleep.

The song continued unvarying in the still night. The absurdity of the whole week became suddenly typified for me in that situation – my preposterous clothes, the sleeping animals, and the wakeful party on the other side of the stockade.

First Nightmare

When we have been home from abroad for a week or two, and time after time, in answer to our friends' polite inquiries, we have retold our experiences, letting phrase engender phrase, until we have made quite a good story of it all; when the unusual people we encountered have, in retrospect, become fabulous and fantastic, and all the checks and uncertainties of travel had become very serious dangers; when the minor annoyances assume heroic proportions and have become, at the luncheon-table, barely endurable privations; even before that, when in the later stages of our journey we reread in our diaries the somewhat bald chronicle of the preceding months – how very little attention do we pay, among all these false frights and bogies, to the stark horrors of boredom.

It seems to me that not nearly enough has been said about this aspect of travel. No one can have any conception of what boredom really means until he has been to the tropics. The boredom of civilized life is trivial and terminable, a puny thing to be strangled between finger and thumb. The blackest things in European social life – rich women talking about their poverty, poor women talking about their wealth, week-end parties of Cambridge aesthetes or lecturers from the London School of Economics, rival Byzantinists at variance, actresses off the stage, psychologists explaining one's own books to one, Americans explaining how much they have drunk lately, house-flies at early morning in the South of France, amateur novelists talking about royalties and reviews, amateur journalists, quarrelling lovers, mystical atheists, raconteurs, dogs, Jews conversant with the group movements of Montparnasse, people who try to look inscrutable, the very terrors, indeed, which drive one to refuge in the still-remote regions of the earth, are mere pansies and pimpernels to the rank flowers which flame grossly in those dark and steaming sanctuaries.

I am constitutionally a martyr to boredom, but never in Europe have I been so desperately and degradingly bored as I was during the next four days; they were as black and timeless as Damnation; a handful of fine ashes thrown into the eyes, a blanket over the face, a mass of soft clay knee deep. My diary reminds me of my suffering in those very words, but the emotion which prompted them seems remote. I know a woman who is always having babies; every time she resolves that that one shall be the last. But, every time, she forgets her resolution, and it is only when her labour begins that she cries to midwife and husband, 'Stop, stop; I've just remembered what it is like. I refuse to have another.' But it is then too late. So the human race goes on. Just in this way, it seems to me, the activity of our ant-hill is preserved by a merciful process of oblivion. 'Never again,' I say on the steps of the house, 'never again will I lunch with that woman.' 'Never again,' I say in the railway carriage, 'will I go and stay with those people.'

And yet a week or two later the next invitation finds me eagerly accepting. 'Stop,' I cry inwardly, as I take my hostess's claw-like hand. 'Stop, stop,' I cry in my tepid bath; 'I have just remembered what it is like. I refuse to have another.' But it is too late.

From time to time I meet people who say they are never bored; they are of two kinds; both, for the most part, liars. Some are equally entranced by almost all observable objects, a straggle of blossom on a white-washed wall, chimneys against the sky, two dogs on a muck heap, an old man with a barrow . . . Precepts of my house master, a very indolent clergyman, rise before me . . . 'only a dull boy is ever dull' . . . 'the world is so full of a number of things' . . .

Others find consolation in their own minds. Whenever they are confronted with a dreary prospect, they tell me, they just slip away from the barren, objective world into the green pastures and ivory palaces of imagination. Perhaps, by a kind of arrested development, some of them really have retained this happy faculty of childhood, but as a rule I find that both these boasts boil down to a simple form of pessimism – the refusal to recognize that any particular human activity can be of greater value than any other one.

Has anyone ever compiled an anthology of bored verse? It would make a pretty Christmas book with Richard Sickert's 'Ennui' as Frontispiece. Shakespeare and the Bible are full of passages that might be quoted; then there is Mr Herbert's housemaid's song from *Riverside Nights*, and the wartime 'Nobody knows how bored we are, and nobody seems to care'. There might be an appendix of suicides' letters which appear constantly in the daily Press and are too soon forgotten, confessions of faith by men in early middle age who say: *'I am fed up and have resolved to end it all. It just goes on and on. Yesterday the clock broke and there is four shillings owing for the milk. Tell Ruby the key of the coal-cellar is under the hat upstairs. There is not any coal. I have not been a bad man, but I couldn't stand it. Give Aunt Loo my love; she was always one of the best. If the milkman says it's more, it is only four shillings.'*

I wish I could write an account worthy of inclusion in that anthology of the four days between Harar and Aden, but the truth is that they have become vague and insignificant. The suffering was genuine enough, but like a mother emerging from twilight sleep, I am left with only the vague impression that nothing much happened.

Nothing much happened. After luncheon I paid off my mules, the guide, the porter, and the old man who had, by sheer persistence at some indefined moment during the journey, become recognized as a legitimate member of my suite.

Then I sat in Mr Bollolakos' hotel.

Outside in the empty streets the white dust lay radiant and miasmic. Inside there was shade. The bar was locked; the servants were all asleep. The courtyard was unendurable. There was only one place to sit – a small square parlour with cement floor and whitewashed walls; in the centre a table with a plush cloth over it, against the walls a rickety wicker couch and two iron rocking-chairs. I had nothing to read except the first volume of a pocket edition of Pope. There are moments when one does not want to read Pope; when one requires something bulky and informative. There was no bookshop or newsagent in the town. Most hotels, however simple, harbour some reading-matter of some sort or other: brochures of advertisement, magazines or novels left by previous visitors, a few postcards on a rack . . . At Mr Bollolakos' there was nothing.

For an hour or two I sat in the rocking-chair reading Pope's juvenile poems.

Most of the time I thought about how awful the next day would be.

In my bedroom were three more volumes of Pope and some writing-paper.

But I should have to cross the courtyard to get to my bedroom.

Presently I got more uninterested in Pope's juvenile poems and decided to cross the courtyard. The three volumes of Pope were somewhere at the bottom of my bag; but I found the writing-paper quite easily; also a minute French dictionary I had forgotten about.

I sat for an hour or so and read the French dictionary, rocking the iron chair in the parlour. '*Bourrasque*, f., squall; fit. *Bourre*, f., wadding; trash. *Bourreau*, m., executioner.' . . .

Presently I drew the table up to the wicker couch, rolled back the plush covering, and wrote a great many letters of Christmas greetings to everyone in England whose address I could remember. I said that it was lovely in Abyssinia; that I pitied them in the fogs and monotony of London; that I longed to see them again and hear all their scandal; that I should be home early in the New Year; that I had bought them presents of shocking

Abyssinian painting, which I would deliver on my return to England – every word was a lie.

At sunset the servants woke up; the bar was opened; tables were brought out into the courtyard and laid for dinner; Mr and Mrs Hall and the Cypriot bank-manager arrived. I told them that I had no books, and they compassionately lent me some copies of *John o' London's Weekly*. Mr Hall was most amiable. He led me back to his house after dinner and showed me some pastel drawings he had made of Ethiopian sunsets, and a coloured photograph of the Prince of Wales which stood on a draped easel in a corner of the drawing-room. His invitation for the coronation had arrived by yesterday's mail; intrigue in high places had delayed it, he said; there were many members of the commercial community who were jealous of his wife's jewellery; and he nodded significantly to the fine brooch commemorating the opening of Epping Forest to the public.

That night, under my mosquito curtain, I read three issues of *John o' London's Weekly* straight through, word for word, from cover to cover.

Next morning after breakfast I read the fourth. Then I went up to the bank and dragged out the cashing of a small cheque to the utmost limits of politeness; I sent a letter of introduction to the famous M. de Montfried, but learned that he was in Europe. It was still early in the day. I took a dose of sleeping-draught and went to bed again.

That evening the train from Hawash arrived, bringing the old gentleman with whom I had travelled to Addis Ababa and one of the ladies who had been staying at the legation. He was on his way to visit the Plowmans at Harar; she was going to the coast and then to Europe. The latest news from Addis was that everyone felt very tired.

Early next morning the train left for Djibouti. There was none of the formality or facility that had characterized our arrival. Half an hour after the train was due to start, the lady from the legation and I were turned out of the carriages which she had occupied on the previous two days, to make room for the servants of an Abyssinian princess who was running down to the coast for a little shopping. These men were very drunk and employed their time in throwing beer-bottles into the desert from the observation platform. With every mile of the journey the heat and humidity became worse; the country on either side of the line was unrelieved emptiness; we rattled and jolted very slowly along the narrow track, increasing by another hour and a half the delay which the royal party had caused, while the young lady from the legation entertained me with censorious comments on the two or three English and Irish acquaintances whom we found in common.

There was one moment of excitement when, towards sundown, we came in sight of the sea and saw that the *Général Voyron* was still there. She lay far out in the harbour, with steam up, presumably waiting for the train. The line into Djibouti turns and twists among great boulders and dry watercourses, so that sometimes we lost sight of her for ten minutes at a time; with every reappearance she seemed further away. Presently it became clear that she had, in fact, already sailed.

I discussed the question with the Messageries agent, but he was unpenitent. I had said in my telegram that I was coming at five-thirty; he had kept the ship back until six; I had arrived at seven; it was not his affair that the train was late; sometimes on that line trains were several days late. This attitude is described, by those who like it, as Latin logic. It is true that Armenians do not see things in the same terms.

We went to the Hôtel des Arcades. Madame's geniality seemed less comforting than it had done on my first arrival. We visited the British vice-consul to ask about ships and learned that there was one to Europe on Thursday and a small boat to Aden on Saturday; the next Messageries ship to Zanzibar left in a fortnight; he said that there had been several little earthquakes during the last month and showed us a large fissure in the wall of his office.

I returned to the hotel in low spirits. From any point of view the prospect seemed unsatisfactory. The primary need seemed to be immediate escape from Djibouti. I had practically made up my mind to return to Europe when Madame at the hotel came to my rescue. There was an Italian boat leaving for Aden next day; the Messageries ship from Zanzibar would pick me up there. We dined on the pavement and I went to bed more hopefully.

Next day was the most deadly of all. I was awakened at dawn with information that the Italian boat was in, and was leaving in an hour. I dressed in haste, fastened my luggage, and hurried downstairs. Madame greeted me in a pink *peignoir*. The boy had made a mistake. There was no boat in.

As soon as it was open I went to the Italian shipping office and bought my ticket. Their ship was due at any time, and would leave within an hour or two of her arrival. She was called the *Somalia*. They would ring me up at the hotel as soon as she was sighted. I sat about the hotel all day waiting for their message; it was impossible to go far away. We visited the chief store of the town and bought some books; the Abyssinian princess was there in a heavy green veil, bargaining over a pseudo-Chinese dinner-gong of atrocious construction. At dinnertime the shipping company rang up to say that the *Somalia* was not expected until next morning. Later that evening I discovered that there were three American cinema-men staying at the other hotel; their company was very pleased with them for the pictures they had made of the coronation, and they were very pleased with themselves. We went for an exquisitely dismal jaunt together in the native town.

Next day was pretty bad. I was again called at dawn with the news that the *Somalia* was in and would sail directly. This time the information was partially correct. I paid, in my haste without questioning it, an hotel bill of staggering size, and hurried down to the sea. The *Somalia* was there all right, a clean little coastal steamer with accommodation for half a dozen passengers. When I had embarked I learned that she was not sailing until six that evening. I had not the spirit to return to the shore; I watched the liner for Europe arrive, take up the lady from the legation, and steam away. All that day I sat on a swivel chair in the saloon, reading one of the books I had purchased at the store – a singularly ill-informed account of Abyssinia, translated from the English.

Eventually, rather after six o'clock, we sailed, and crossed in fine weather to Aden. There were five of us at dinner that night – the captain, a French clerk, and an Italian official and his wife on their way to Mogadishu. We had nothing much to say to each other. The Italian official made some jokes about seasickness; the French clerk gave me some figures, whose significance I have now forgotten, about the coffee trade at Hodeida; the captain was gallant in Italian to the official's wife.

Next morning we arrived at Aden. That was the end of four exceedingly painful days.

PENGUIN SPECIAL
The Life and Times of Allen Lane
Jeremy Lewis

Penguin Special is the story of how a stocky, 'unbookish' Bristolian went on to found the most famous publishing house in the world. As well as providing a comprehensive account of Allen Lane's achievements both as the founder and head of a company that had a major influence on the life of post-war Britain, Jeremy Lewis's highly entertaining biography also reveals a mischievous, often contradictory and oddly endearing figure who loathed meetings and paperwork, insisted on the best writers and academics despite his own lack of formal education, and struggled to come to terms with the 1960s Britain that Penguin itself had helped to usher in. Published on the occasion of Penguin's 70th birthday, *Penguin Special* is a superlative portrait of the greatest publisher of the twentieth century.

May 2005 ISBN 0670914851 £25

PENGUIN BY DESIGN
A Cover Story 1935–2005
Phil Baines

Published to coincide with Penguin's 70th birthday and a major display at the V&A, *Penguin by Design* is a celebration of the rich and diverse design heritage of Penguin book covers. Beautifully illustrated throughout and written by a leading design writer, *Penguin by Design* is required reading for anybody interested not only in the evolution of the Penguin brand but also in the development of British publishing and graphic design as a profession.

June 2005 ISBN 0713998393 £15

To order a copy of either of these books, simply call Penguin Books c/o Bookpost on **01624 677237** and have your credit/debit card ready. Alternatively e-mail your order to bookshop@enterprise.net Postage and package is free in mainland UK. Overseas customers must add £2 per book. Price and availability subject to change without notice.